In the Footsteps of Lafcadio Hearn aka Koizumi Yakumo

PROLOGUE

Lafcadio is highly revered in Japan for writing about Japanese legends, folktales and traditions, during a time of disruptive high-speed modernization (Meiji era) and for introducing the culture and literature of his adopted country to the west.

Actually, there is much more to Lafcadio's life and literature than his writings about Japan.

He was born on the Greek island of Lefcada in 1850 to a Greek mother and an Irish father. He was abandoned by both his parents to the care of a wealthy grandaunt and grew up in Ireland. He was educated in England and in France, ended up penniless at seventeen and emigrated to the USA at the age of nineteen. He worked as a journalist, translated French authors into English and wrote numerous newspaper articles and few books before moving to Japan at the age of forty. He got married in Japan and took his wife's family name (Koizumi).

This travelogue is a slightly edited version of my Facebook posts (2021/2022). I start from Lefcada and the other Ionian Islands, then to Ireland, France and England, to New York, Cincinnati, New Orleans and the island of Martinique (in the Caribbean). I follow Lafcadio's trip back to New York, then by train from Montreal through most of Canada to Vancouver and by steamship to Yokohama. From there to Matsue, Kumamoto, Kobe, Tokyo and Yaizu. I write snippets of history along the way and show pictures as I am retracing Lafcadio's footsteps.

I have used numerous sources of information and I have tried to distil the most interesting stories into just few sentences. A significant part of what I have written about Lafcadio's life is from what I have heard from Takis Efstathiou and what I have read in Paul Murray's book. Takis, a fine arts dealer in New York, has been an indefatigable promoter of Lafcadio's open mind in Greece, Ireland and the USA for two dozen years. Paul Murray, a former Irish diplomat, wrote an exceptionally well researched biography: *A Fantastic Journey: The Life and Literature of Lafcadio Hearn.*

By interposing some of my personal experiences at the various locations and some historical tidbits, I have attempted to provide an informative and entertaining narrative.

John Vlachopoulos

Burlington, Ontario, Canada

John Vlachopoulos, *In the Footsteps of Lafcadio Hearn aka Koizumi Yakumo Polydynamics Inc, Canada (2022)*

ISBN 978-0-9952407-4-2 (Book)

ISBN 978-0-9952407-5-9 (Electronic book)

Published by:

POLYDYNAMICS INC, Dundas, ON, CANADA

www.polydynamics.com

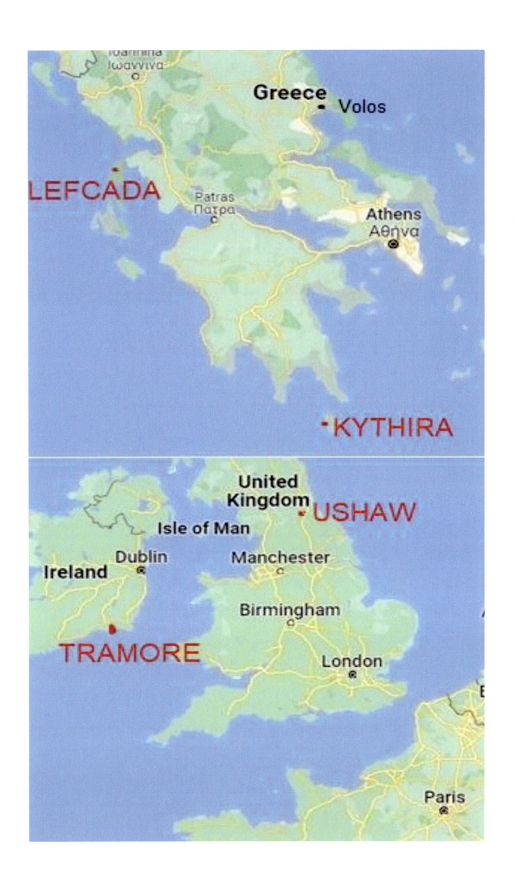

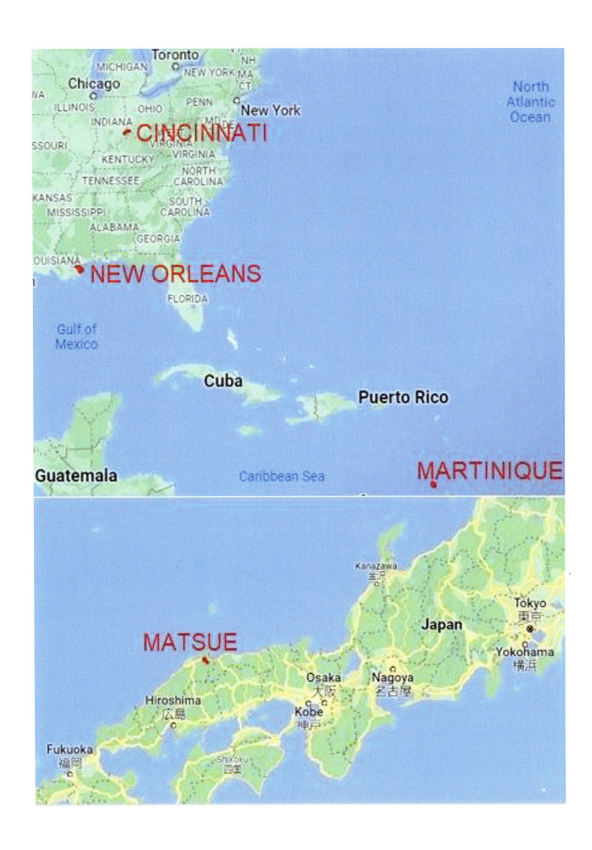

LOCATION page

Lafcadio's birthplace
LEFCADA, GREECE

Lefcada is the birthplace of Patrick Lafcadio Hearn (Πατρίκιος Λευκάδιος Χερν) aka Koizumi Yakumo (1850-1904). His mother was Greek (Rosa Antoniou Cassimati) and his father Irish (Surgeon-Major Charles Bush Hearn). Charles took his young family to Dublin, where eventually Lafcadio was abandoned by both his parents, to the care of his wealthy aunt Sarah Holmes Brenane. After going to school in France and Ireland, Lafcadio emigrated to USA (New York, Cincinnati and New Orleans), lived for a couple of years in Martinique and then moved to Japan, where he became very famous for his stories and books on Japanese culture and folklore.

In Matsue, Japan, he married Koizumi Setsu, became a Japanese citizen and took the name Koizumi Yakumo. A museum in his name opened in 1933 and his residence was declared a historical site in 1940. A museum called "Historical Center of Lafcadio Hearn" was inaugurated in Lefcada on June 4, 2014. It contains rare books, Japanese collectibles, photographs and other exhibits donated by New York art dealer Takis Efstathiou. I am starting from Lefcada for my travelogue and I hope that you enjoy the ride as much as I do.

According to mythology, poetess Sappho committed suicide by jumping off a cliff in the south of the island, for having been rejected by her handsome boatman lover Phaon. The naval battle of Actium was fought in the Ionian Sea between Lefcada and Actium, which is just 15 kilometers north east on the mainland of Greece. Octavian (later known as Augustus Caesar) defeated the combined fleet of Mark Antony and Cleopatra in 31 BC. The battle of Actium marks Rome's transition from Republic to Empire.

Lefcada and the rest of the Ionian Islands were under Venetian rule for hundreds of years and after a brief occupation by the French, they became a British protectorate from about 1810 to 1864. In fact, a great-great-grandfather of Camilla, Duchess of Cornwall, had served as governor of the Ionian Island of Zante (Ζάκυνθος). So, both Prince Charles (Prince Philip was born on Corfu) and the Duchess have Ionian Islands connections.

Skorpios was a barren island when purchased by Aristotle Onassis in 1963. The greenery in the picture is due to over 200 species of plants and trees imported. It is situated at about 2 kilometers from the resort town of Nidri, in the strait between Lefcada and mainland Greece. Onassis married Jacqueline Bouvier Kennedy on Skorpios in 1968.

The new owner Ekaterina Rybolovleva (born in 1989) married Uruguayan businessman and politician Juan Sartori in 2015, also on the island. I hired a motorboat and went around Skorpios in August of 2016, but there did not seem to be anyone there, except for a few guards. Ekaterina's father, Russian oligarch Dmitry Rybolovlev, has planned facilities of "Davos-like standards," for hosting conferences for "ultra high net work individuals"

KYTHIRA

Avlemonas
2011.09.01

Antikythira Mechanism

Kythira is the birthplace of Lafcadio Hearn's mother, Rosa Antoniou Cassimati. Although not in the vicinity of the other Ionian Islands, it is traditionally considered as one of the seven islands (Επτάνησα). It is located where the Ionian Sea meets the Aegean, just south of the Peloponnese and northwest of Crete. Together with the other "Seven-Islands" it was a British protectorate. Lafcadio's father, Dr. Charles Hearn (later Surgeon-Major), was accompanying his regiment for duty on Cerigo (as Kythira was known at the time) and soon after his arrival he met Rosa.

The island's history goes back to mythological times. It competes with Cyprus, for the title of the birthplace of Aphrodite, the goddess of love. Due to its central location, it has attracted merchants, sailors, colonists, invaders, conquerors and pirates over the centuries. Apparently, there was a Phoenician settlement at Avlemonas, before the time of Classical Greece. It had been occupied by Athens and Sparta in the 5th and 4th centuries BC. After the capture, looting and pillaging of Constantinople in 1204, by the Crusaders, it was ruled by Venice, and that is how it acquired the name Cerigo. Hayreddin Barbarossa (son of an Ottoman father and a Greek mother) captured Cerigo in 1537, caused a lot of destruction and sold many of the inhabitants as slaves in Africa. Rule by Venice was fully restored after the Battle of Lepanto (Ναύπακτος,1571). After the fall of the Venetian Republic to Napoleon (1797), Cerigo and the other islands were briefly under French and Russian control before becoming a British protectorate from about 1815 to 1864.

Some 35 km south of Kythira is Antikythera, famous for being the location of a shipwreck, from which the Antikythira Mechanism and the statue of Ephebe (Youth), dated to 2nd or 3rd century BC, were recovered (1900). The Mechanism (13 centimeters in diameter) is usually described as the world's first computer, capable of calculating astronomical positions and the eclipses of sun and moon, many years in advance. There are some inaccuracies due to limitations of the available planetary theory at the time of construction. It was not a unique device, but rather one of a few such mechanisms built during the 2nd and 3rd centuries BC. However, the world had to wait for over a thousand years for a device of such mechanical complexity to be constructed again.

The Ephebe or Youth (1.96 meters in height) appears to be holding some kind of a round object. It has been suggested that it depicts Paris, the lover of Helen of Troy, offering the apple of discord to goddess Aphrodite.

Both the Antikythira Mechanism and the Ephebe are now on display at the National Archaeological Museum of Athens. Kythira has not had the explosive tourism development of several other Greek islands, so it has retained its unique island charm. It was renown even in ancient times and more so in the Venetian period for high quality wine, honey and olive oil. I only visited once, in 2011, but I will certainly go back.

KERKYRA (CORFU)

Pontikonisi and Vlacherna Monastery, CORFU

Achilleion Palace Garden, CORFU

Corfu (Kerkyra) with population of over 100,000 is the most populous of the Ionian Islands (Heptanesa). It is steeped in history, rich in culture and endowed with natural beauty. According to Homer's Odyssey, Ulysses was washed up on a beach of the island of the Phaeacians (believed to be present day Corfu) and met Nausica the daughter of King Alkinoos. She took him to the royal palace and arranged for his return to his home island of Ithaca, some 100 kilometers south.

Kerkyra has played a very important role throughout the history of Greece. However, the rule by Venice, which started in 1386 till the French occupation of 1797, has left an indelible mark. It was the only part of Greece that was never conquered by the Ottomans, despite repeated attempts. Venetians, Greeks, foreign mercenaries and their strong fortifications withstood and repulsed all assaults. Under the Venetian rule of 400 years, the Corfiotes developed an intense interest in music, theater and opera. The accolade "applaudito in Corfú" had a special meaning for operatic performers.

The **Achilleion** Palace had been built by Kaiserin Elisabeth (Sisi) of Austria in 1889. She was grieving after the murder-suicide of her only son Rudolf, with his seventeen-year-old girlfriend Mary von Vetsera (daughter of Eleni Baltazzi of Chios, Smyrna and Constantinople) at Mayerling. After Elisabeth's assassination in Geneva (1898), Achilleion was sold to Kaiser Wilhelm II. At another summer palace, called Mon Repos, Prince Philip was born in 1921.

Several other notable people were born or lived in Corfu, including Ioannis Kapodistrias, the first governor of modern Greece, writer Lawrence Durrell and his naturalist brother Gerald. Lafcadio Hearn's mother Rosa Antoniou Cassimati died at a psychiatric hospital in Corfu in 1882.

There is even a connection between Corfu and the village of Ancaster, Ontario located just 7 km from McMaster University: British army officer Otto Ives had fought against the Ottomans during the war of Greek independence and married Magdalene Diamanti, in Corfu, before arriving and settling in Ancaster, Ontario, in 1832. Magdalene's younger sister (or niece) Angeliki also came along and lived with the couple in a large house, called the Hermitage. She did not speak much English and Otto Ives's coachman, William Black, was teaching her the language. Black fell in love with the Greek girl and asked Ives for permission to marry.

According to the legend, Ives vehemently told him that a coachman was not worthy of marrying the sister of a British colonel's wife and whose father was the governor of the Ionian Island of Paxoi (just 10 km south of Corfu). Very disappointed, William Black decided to end his life and his body was found hanging in the barn, next morning. A road near the property is called 'Lovers Lane' and the ruins of the house and barn are supposed to be haunted, occasionally visited by aficionados of ghost stories. Lafcadio would love this story and if he had heard about it, he would have written a book.

KEFALONIA and ITHACA

Myrtos beach, Kefalonia

Paliki

Kefalonia

Ithaki

Kefalonia is the largest of the Ionian islands and ITHACA the second smallest of the seven (Heptanisa). The question is whether modern Ithaca is Homer's Ithaki (Ἰθάκη), the home of Ulysses (Odysseus). He was the brains behind the Trojan horse ploy. It took ten years for him to return from Troy to his Ithaki island-home and to his wife Penelope, according to Homer's Odyssey. Of course, Homer was composing poetry, not writing history. Was it all fiction? legends and myths? or was there some historical basis embellished with poetic license?

Archeologists in the 1800s were sceptical and ridiculed Heinrich Schliemann's obsession to search for Troy and Mycenae. Many have blamed him for his amateurish excavation methods, but no one can argue with Schliemann's success. Even though the battle of Troy took place in the 13th century BC and Homer wrote the Iliad and Odyssey in the 8th century BC, Ulysses was probably a real person. The search for Ulysses' Ithaki has been going on for over two thousand years and has been intensified after Schliemann unearthed Troy (near Hissarlik in modern Turkey) and Mycenae in the Peloponnese.

The archaeological evidence favours present day Ithaca. Homer's geographical description favours the Paliki peninsula of Kefalonia. Paliki was an island, three thousand years ago, separated by a narrow channel in the west side, while Ithaca is separated by a less than a 4 km wide straight, in the east of Kefalonia.

The Ulyssean heritage seems to have influenced the psyche of Kefalonians and those of the surrounding islands. They are reputed to travel, emigrate and settle in faraway places. The first Greek to set foot in Canada was Ioannis Fokas from Kefalonia, better known by his hispanized name Juan de Fuca. He led a Spanish expedition in 1592 in search of the legendary passage, believed to link Atlantic and Pacific. The **Juan de Fuca Straight** is a 150 km long channel, 20-40 km wide, separating Canada's Vancouver island, from the USA.

Another famous Kefalonian was Constantine Gerakis (his family name means falcon in English, Faucon in French). He franco-anglicized his family name to PHAULKON and arrived in Siam (modern day Thailand) in 1675 working for England's East India Company. In addition to his native Greek, he could speak English, French, Portuguese and became fluent in the Siamese language in a couple of years. He worked first as interpreter for King Narai the Great, eventually became the king's chief councillor and some sort of de facto prime minister. When the king became terminally ill rumours spread that Phaulkon was planning to rule the country with the designated heir to the throne as a puppet king. A military coup ensued led by one of the mandarins, the heir to the throne and Phaulkon were arrested, tortured and executed in 1688.

Lefcada is situated less than 10 km north of Ithaki. So, it is not surprising that Lafcadio Hearn embarked on his own Odyssey to Ireland, France, England, New York, Cincinnati, New Orleans, Martinique and Japan in the late 1800s and wrote about his experiences.

ZAKYNTHOS (ZANTE)

Navagio, ZAKYNTHOS

Zakynthos (called **Zante** by the Venetians) is a large Ionian island situated 10 km south of Kefalonia and 20 km west of the Peloponnese. In Homer's Odyssey (translated by Samuel Butler) Ulysses says "I live in Ithaki, where there is a high mountain…. covered with forests;

and not far from it there is a group of islands very near to one another... and the wooded island of Zakynthos. It [Ithaki] lies squat on the horizon, all highest up in the sea towards the sunset, while the others lie away from it towards dawn". This passage led to speculation that present day Ithaca is not Homer's Ithaki, because it is supposed to be "towards the sunset, Gr. πρὸς ζόφον" whereas modern Ithaca is east of Kefalonia.

Zakynthos played a very significant role in the Greek War of Independence (1821-1829) mainly because of two men: Pre-eminent revolutionary leader Theodoros Kolokotronis and British army officer Richard Church. Kolokotronis was the scion of a powerful clan in the Peloponnese. He became a klepht (warrior-bandit) at an early age and the Ottomans put a price on his head. Fearing capture and/or assassination, he fled to Zakynthos in 1806, which was under French control. In 1810 British troops occupied Zakynthos and Irish born Richard Church raised the 1st Regiment Greek Light Infantry. Kolokotronis was recruited and quickly promoted to the rank of Major under the command of Colonel Church. Richard Church with his Greek regiment took part in several battles (mostly against the French) and became "more Greek than the Greeks". He travelled to the Vienna Congress in 1815 and argued in favor of the Greek cause for independence.

The training received by Kolokotronis, for at least 6 years, was invaluable when he returned to Peloponnese. He managed to convince the quarrelsome warlords and to organize the undisciplined klephts to fight like an army rather than as fiercely independent bandits. He used to wear the ceremonial crested red helmet of the 1st Regiment during the battles. Church and Kolokotronis developed a close friendship and maintained correspondence. After the establishment of the Greek free state, Church was invited and came to Greece a couple of times before becoming a Greek citizen in 1834, army General and Senator. He died in 1873, aged 90 and was buried at the 1st Cemetery of Athens.

Zakynthos and the other Ionian islands were under British rule till 1864. Lt.-Col. John Whitehill Parsons, great-great-grandfather of Camilla, Duchess of Cornwall, served as British Resident (governor) of Zakynthos. He died in Corfu in 1848.

Irish born Dr. Charles Bush Hearn, Lafcadio's father, served as surgeon in several regiments in Zakynthos, Ithaca and Corfu between 1845 and 1848, in terms lasting "from six months to one year". He was transferred to Kythira in 1848 and to Lefcada in 1849.

DUBLIN, IRELAND

Trinity College, Dublin, Ireland

Trinity College (University of Dublin) was founded by Queen Elizabeth I in 1592. Although situated in the very heart of Dublin, the campus is an island of tranquility. I did not search in any maps for the university, but as I was walking along Grafton Street (which is the principal commercial street), I ended up inside the campus (May 2000).

The long list of notable graduates includes writers Oscar Wilde, Jonathan Swift, Bram Stoker, Samuel Beckett and mathematician W. R. Hamilton (known for Hamiltonian mechanics, Cayley-Hamilton theorem and much more). The Old Library holds many thousands of rare books and it is a tourist attraction. Lafcadio's father, Charles Bush Hearn (1818-1866) received a B.A. from Trinity before studying medicine at the Royal College of Surgeons in Dublin.

He was born in Lefcada, on June 27, 1850 and was baptized 12 days later as Patrick Lafcadio, in the absence of his father, who had been reassigned to the island of Dominica in the Caribbean. As a two-year old, he travelled with his mother Rosa and his uncle Richard (Charles younger bother) to Ireland, arriving at the Anglo-Irish Hearn home in Rathmines, a suburb of Dublin, on August 1, **1852**. He never returned to Greece, but he always identified with his Greek lineage. Later in life, he wrote: 'Being of a meridional race myself, a Greek, I feel with the Latin race than with the Anglo-Saxon'.

Rosa's life was not a happy one in Lefcada or in Dublin. She was married to Charles in a Greek church in Lefcada on November 25, 1849, two months pregnant with her second son (Lafcadio). Her husband left her for his next assignment three months later. Their first child, George Robert, died two months after Lafcadio's birth, in August 1850. In Ireland, her knowledge of Greek and Italian was of no use and she had real difficulty learning English. The absence of her husband, limited communication with her in-laws and the Dublin weather (definitely not like her sun-drenched Greek island) led to a nervous breakdown.

Her husband returned in October of 1853, but he left again for the Crimean war six months later. Rosa returned to Kythira in the summer of 1854 and gave birth to their third son James Daniel in August. She never returned to Ireland and Charles had their marriage annulled. In Kythira she married Giovanni Cavallini and had four more children. James was dispatched to his Irish relatives in Dublin and never saw his mother again.

Lafcadio was left to the care of Charles' wealthy maternal aunt Sarah Brenane, who had converted from Protestantism to Catholicism. His father returned in 1856, got married to a widowed old flame of his and left for an assignment to India in the summer of 1957, never to return. Lafcadio never saw his mother after the age of four or his father after the age of seven. He lived a life of privilege, taught by private tutors and had summer vacations at **Tramore**, in the southeast coast of Ireland.

PARIS, FRANCE

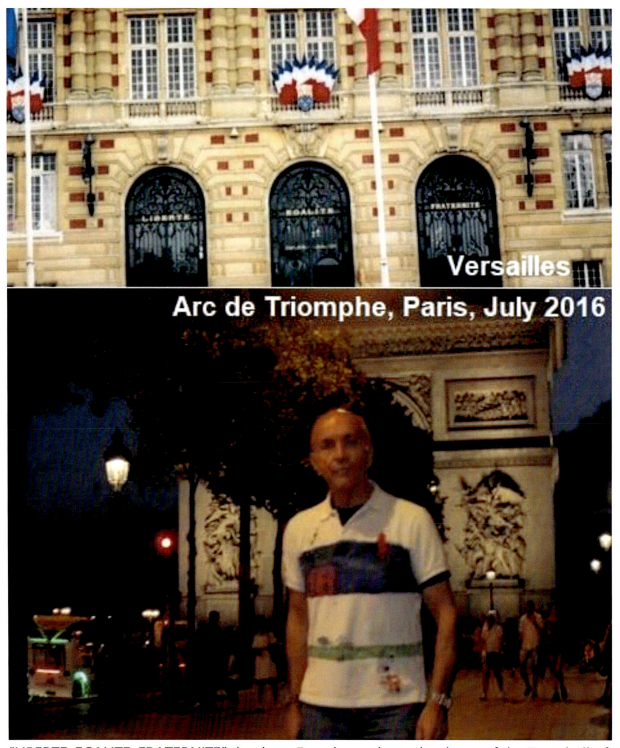

Versailles

Arc de Triomphe, Paris, July 2016

"LIBERTE, EGALITE, FRATERNITE" the three French words on the doors of the Townhall of

Versailles, were apparently expressed together for the first time in a speech by Robespierre, during the French Revolution. The famous phrase "Qu'ils mangent de la brioche" or "Laissez-les manger du gâteau" (let them eat cake) was never uttered by Marie Antoinette, but it is a myth that defined the deplorable social inequalities and living conditions in France, in the late 1700s. She probably had no clue that the vast majority of people in Paris could not afford to buy a loaf of bread. The clergy and the nobility, no more than 3% of the population, were ruling and exploiting the masses.

The **French Revolution** is one of the most important events in the history of the Western World. On **July 14, 1789** a large mob attacked Bastille, a royal fortress with stores of arms and ammunition, which was also used as a prison. Quatorze Juliet is the National Day of France. The Revolution was followed by the Reign of Terror, when tens of thousands, of suspected "counter-revolutionaries" were brutally exterminated. The fate of King Louis XVI, Marie Antoinette and Robespierre is well known, but the events surrounding Lavoisier's execution are not.

Antoine Lavoisier is considered as the father of modern chemistry. He is known for discovering the role of oxygen in combustion and for changing chemistry from a qualitative art to a quantitative science. He was a French aristocrat and his family-owned large amount of land. I am copying from the book of P. Cane and S. Nisenson "Giants of Science" Pyramid books (1959). "Lavoisier had the misfortune to incur the wrath of Jean Paul Marat, one of the leaders of the Terror following the French Revolution, because Lavoisier had rejected a chemical treatise submitted by Marat to the French Academy of Science. Marat denounced the scientist and succeeded in requesting the arrest.............. All petitions to free Lavoisier as a great scientist who had rendered invaluable services to the state failed. On May 8, 1794, the guillotine ended his life".

Lavoisier's student and apprentice Éleuthère I. **DuPont**, fearing the worst, sailed for a new life in the USA and arrived with his family on January 1, 1800. He founded a gunpowder company, which became one of the most successful American corporations known as E. I. du Pont de Nemours or simply DuPont (currently over 100,000 employees in various divisions and spin-offs, worldwide).

Lafcadio studied in England at a Roman Catholic boarding school (known as Ushaw College) founded by seminarians who had left France during the French Revolution. He spent also some time in France in the 1860s, but where and when it is not known. He acquired excellent knowledge of the French language as a teenager and made masterful translations of Guy de Maupassant, Flaubert and Gautier, later on. Yone Noguchi in his 1910 book 'Lafcadio Hearn in Japan' wrote **"His Greek temperament and French culture became frost-bitten as a flower in the North."**

USHAW COLLEGE, UK

Ushaw College Library, 1800s

Lafcadio,Ushaw,1866

Ushaw College Library, 2000s County Durham, England

Lafcadio Hearn was taught by a private tutor at home, when he was living with his wealthy grandaunt, in Ireland, till about the age of 13. There is some evidence that he was also educated in France, but no school records are available. In September 1863 he arrived at the Roman Catholic boarding school known as Ushaw College, County Durham, in northern England. He was there for four years, with little time away on vacation.

Lafcadio was not fond of the strict discipline and religious indoctrination, but he was appreciative of fitness activities. At 16 he was struck on his left eye by the rotating rope of a swing called 'Giants Stride'. Infection resulted in complete loss of left eyesight. Also, the slight disfigurement made him want to have his picture taken only from the right side of his face.

Ushaw College was an off-shoot of the English School of Douai, in northern France. The English School was a seminary established by Roman Catholics who fled from England during the reign of **Queen Elizabeth I**. Troubles for them had started with Elizabeth's father **Henry VIII**. He was obsessed with having a male heir to the throne and he wanted to divorce his wife Catherine of Aragon and marry Ann Boleyn. The Pope refused to grant annulment, so Henry declared himself Supreme Head of the Church of England and got married to Anne. Henry's trusted advisor and Chancellor, Sir Thomas More, refused to acknowledge the 'supremacy' of the king and the annulment of his marriage. He was convicted of treason and beheaded just outside the Tower of London.

Elizabeth's mother, **Ann Boleyn**, was convicted for 'incest and adultery' and beheaded at about the same location, a year later. A few years after Henry died (1547), his first daughter Mary I, became queen. She was Catholic like her mother Catherine and started to reverse the Protestant reforms. After an uprising some 300 were burned at stake and that is why she got the moniker "Bloody Mary". After her death, Elizabeth became queen with the support of the Protestants. During an uprising by Catholics some 700 were brutally executed on Queen's orders. Obviously, English Catholics had good reasons to flee from England and establish their seminary in France during Elizabeth's reign, and then had to flee from France during the French Revolution.

Lafcadio remained at Upshaw till 1867, but he was forced to leave without completing his secondary education. His wealthy grandaunt, Mrs. Brenane, had transferred thousands of acres of land to a certain distant cousin, Henry Hearn Molyneux, who went bankrupt and the property was forfeited. She could no longer afford to pay for boarding and tuition fees for her grandnephew at Ushaw. Lafcadio was forced to live in poverty in **London** at the home of a former maid of Mrs. Brenane, who had married to a dock worker. After having lived in luxury with his grandaunt, taught by private tutors and educated at one of the most prestigious schools, Lafcadio found himself living a Dickensian existence near Thames.

NEW YORK, USA

S. S. Cella at London

t is truly designated the age, the sex, and the occupation of ea

of which it is intended by each to become an inhabitant; and th

died.

18

or Manifest OF ALL THE PASSENGERS taken on boar

Patrick Hearn   19   m   none   Truee

In **1869**, after having spent two years of miserable existence in London, Lafcadio was offered a one-way steerage ticket to **New York**, by the man who had disastrously mismanaged his grandaunt's wealth. Apparently, Henry Molyneux wanted to dispatch Patrick Hearn to America so that he would inherit all of Mrs. Brenane's remaining property. He was 19 (occupation: none, country: Greece) when he arrived in New York, as indicated in the List or Manifest of **S. S. Cella** and from his fully documented birth, on June 27, 1850.

The (volunteer) transcribers at https://heritage.statueofliberty.org typed date of arrival January 1, 1867, in the printed version. My own reading is that it could (and should) be 1869, but I cannot decipher the date and month. Suggestions are welcome. On another trip from West Indies to New York (September 13, 1887) he is listed as 'Lafcadio Hearn, British'.

It was 4 years after the end of the **American Civil War (1861-1865)**. New York had a population of about 1.5 million and rapidly growing. The waves of arriving immigrants were living in apartment buildings called 'tenements'. Typically, they had boarded up windows, leaky plumbing, were overcrowded and disease infested. It was abject poverty not far from city neighborhoods of colossal concentration of wealth of robber barons and financiers, like Cornelius Vanderbilt and J.P. Morgan.

The construction of the Brooklyn Bridge was just starting (completed in 1883). Details of Lafcadio's time in New York are sketchy. He stayed till 1871, doing menial jobs and trying to survive, according to most biographers. Central Park (roughly 1 km x 4 km) was probably where Lefadio would go for go for getting some fresh air. It was a wonderful experience for me jogging in lush greenery surroundings during a few visits.

My own trip from Athens (Piraeus) to New York in 1965, was more like a celebration. I was the recipient of a scholarship (covering living expenses and tuition) for doctoral studies at Washington University, St. Louis, Mo. I was also awarded a Fulbright travel grant for my round-trip ticket. In fact, I was asked if I wanted to travel by air or by sea. I had completed my studies at NTUA (Εθνικό Μετσόβιο Πολυτεχνείο) in July and I sailed on **Queen Frederica** on August 27, 1965.

The ocean liner made stops at Messina, Palermo and Napoli, where we disembarked for about 3-4 hours and I toured the downtown area. The ship also laid anchor a couple of kilometers from Gibraltar. Next stop was Halifax, where I walked around the city for a couple of hours. We arrived in New York in the morning of September 8. The whole trip (better descriptor.... cruise) was an immensely pleasurable experience, swimming and suntanning during the day and partying at night. There were a lot of students aboard, returning to the US from summer vacations in Greece.

CINCINNATI, OH and ST. LOUIS, MO

Lafcadio Hearn at 23 in Cincinnati

John Vlachopoulos at 23 in St.Louis

CINCINNATI
Ohio River

ST. LOUIS
Mississippi River

Lafcadio Hearn left New York in 1871 and arrived in **Cincinnati** to meet a brother-in-law of the man who mismanaged his grandaunt's fortune and who was supposed to help him. He received 5 dollars per week for three weeks. In today's money it would be equivalent to about $100 per week. Life was hard on him and he spent his time doing odd menial jobs to survive and reading in public libraries.

In the 1870s Cincinnati was an industrial city, nicknamed 'Paris of the Americas' for its significant entertainment and cultural activities. The population was about 200,000, most of them of German or Irish descent. The John A. Roebling suspension bridge over Ohio River was completed in 1866. It was named after Johann A. Roebling, a German born and trained engineer, who was also responsible for the initial design and planning of the Brooklyn bridge.

In November of 1872, Lafcadio started receiving payments from the Cincinnati Enquirer for publishing his stories. He was prolific: till the end of that year, he had fifteen stories appear in print, seventy-nine in 1873 and by 1874 he was a full-time reporter and published two hundred and six articles. He realized that for his stories to be popular with the readers of the Enquirer, they had to inform, entertain and shock. He put his extraordinary abilities in writing into overdrive, mostly about the dark side of life. In 1874, the gruesome details, and the evocative language describing the 'Tan-yard murder' which shook the German community, were republished in newspapers across America.

Lafcadio, Paddy Hearn as he was known then, became a local celebrity. Also, in 1874 he got married to Alethea Foley, daughter of a slave woman and her slave owner. Interracial marriage was outlawed in Ohio and he was dismissed from the Enquirer. He was immediately hired by the Cincinnati Commercial and he was their full-time reporter till he left for New Orleans in 1877.

I arrived in **St. Louis** on September 9, 1965. My doctoral research at Washington University involved very high temperature air jets for testing heat shields of space vehicles. The project was of interest to NASA and McDonnell Douglas Corporation, headquartered in St. Louis. However, when I asked whether my computer code would be used in any of the projects related to lunar missions, I received a terse answer "it is classified". Student life was a very intense experience in an atmosphere of hippie counterculture and Vietnam war protests on campus. My picture is from a show on student life aired by a local TV station. The 190-metre Gateway (to the west) Arch was under construction, when I was in St. Louis. I went to the top observation deck, during a visit a couple of years later. I defended my thesis on July 30, 1968 and took up my assistant professor position at McMaster University upon arriving in Hamilton, Ontario, Canada, on August 14. I was promoted through the ranks, served as Department Chair 1985-88 and now I am Professor Emeritus.

NEW ORLEANS

NEW ORLEANS   ST. LOUIS CATHEDRAL

In 1877 Lafcadio decided to abandon his well-paying reporter's job, fame and wife, in Cincinnati and move south to New Orleans. The city was founded in 1718 by the French, where the Mississippi River discharges to the Gulf of Mexico. It remained under French rule for several years, then Spanish and back to French. When Thomas Jefferson's envoys went to Paris to negotiate the purchase of New Orleans with Napoleon (1803), they were told that they had to buy the entire **Louisiana** territory or no deal at all. So, they bought, for $15 million. the huge territory (over 2 million square kilometers) from the Montana border with Canada to New Orleans, nearly doubling the size of what was then the United States. It is without a doubt the largest real estate purchase in the history of the world. And at what a price: about $7 per square kilometer or in today's money about $200, which is less than a dollar per acre!

Slaves were working in cotton and sugar plantations, frequently in abhorrent conditions. However, according to French and Spanish laws, they were allowed to be free on Sundays to go to church or work in other jobs. With money earned they could purchase their freedom, something unheard of in northern states. So, before the American Civil War (1861-1865) perhaps as much as 10% of the free population in New Orleans were former slaves. Those born in Louisiana were called Creoles (white, black or of mixed race), to distinguish them from new arrivals. The multiracial and multilingual society of New Orleans developed a distinct culture reflected in literature, architecture, music and cuisine.

Lafcadio was working as a journalist, translating French authors and writing books. One of them was a cookbook **'La Cuisine Creole'**. Another was 'Chita: A Memory of Last Island' a novella about a young white girl adopted by Spanish parents living on an island southwest of New Orleans, which was completely destroyed during the 1856 hurricane. It was perhaps a foretelling of hurricane Katrina that killed nearly two thousand people in 2005.

He had a very sociable life in New Orleans. His circle of friends included prominent Creoles and local intelligentsia. **Elizabeth Bisland** was the daughter of a plantation owner whose wealth was ruined during the civil war. She was of intimidating beauty and intellect to most men she met, including Lafcadio. They maintained friendship and correspondence for many years. She became a distinguished writer for a New York magazine and wrote a biography of Lafcadio after his death. Rudolph Matas was a young polymath medical doctor of Catalan-Spanish parentage. They became almost like brothers. Lafcadio predicted that Matas would become a great man of medicine. Indeed, Matas had a very distinguished medical career and developed several surgical techniques during his long life, to age 97. He is considered as the 'father of vascular surgery".

I visited New Orleans in 1984 and in 1993 for participation in scientific conferences. During my second visit, I tasted creole cuisine at Antoine's restaurant that has been owned and operated by descendants of the original founder (since 1840).

MARTINIQUE, FRENCH ANTILLES

Lafcadio stayed for two years in Martinique 1887-1889, which was and still is part of France. It is located in the eastern Caribbean Sea. Most of the population (400,000) are Creole descendants of African slaves, mixed with Europeans and native Caribbeans.

Lafcadio settled at St. Pierre which was the commercial and cultural capital of the island. It was frequently called the Paris of the Antilles. In his beautiful illustrated travel book 'Two Years in French West Indies' Lafcadio has a marvellous description of nature "La Montagne Pelee is visible from almost any part of St. Pierre, which nestles in a fold of its rocky skirts....Pelée is grandiose: it spurs out across the island from Caribbean to the Atlantic...Is the great volcano dead?...Nobody knows. Less than forty years ago [1851] it rained ashes over all the roofs of St. Pierre. Within twenty years it has uttered mutterings. For the moment, it appears to sleep"

Unfortunately, Pelée woke up thirteen years later, in 1902. There were explosions, noises, clouds of ash, tremors and earthquakes that frightened the residents of St. Pierre. The warnings continued for two months, but the people believed that their mountain which was referred to as 'Le Volcan Debonaire', was going to have a moderate volcanic activity, like that of 1851. By early May the warnings became more ominous. The French governor formed a committee of five local experts 'to provide scientific opinion, without alarming people'. They concluded that if there was an eruption the lava would flow to a valley and then slowly into the sea. No evacuation was recommended to the residents of St. Pierre.

On May 7 there was a rainstorm, followed by mudslides. The weather cleared and in the morning of May 8 the sky was clear blue. Just before 8.00 AM there was an explosion near the mountain top. Actually, the top itself was solidified lava, which acted like a plug. The enormous power of the volcano was released sideways towards St. Pierre. It was pyroclastic flow ('pyr' in Greek means fire, 'clastic' means fragmented). It was a flow of fiery fragments. Pulverised rock at temperatures reaching 1000 Celsius descended towards St. Pierre at a speed of over hundred of km/hour. Similar eruptions are now called Pelean. The study of the causes and effects marked the beginning of the science of volcanology. It is the deadliest volcanic eruption in recorded history with 30,000 dead in just a few minutes, by fire and the shock wave of the blast. For comparison the Vesuvius eruption of 79 AD, that destroyed Pompeii and Herculaneum, caused about 10,000 deaths.

According to the legend, there were just two survivors at St. Pierre. One of them was a local troublemaker who was in jail and managed to escape during carnival. He was re-arrested after a brawl and placed in solitary confinement in a very small prison cell with meter thick walls and a tiny window. He was badly burned but survived. He became a showman for Barnum and Bailey circus, retelling his story of survival.

NEW YORK

NEW YORK during the GILDED AGE

Gilded Age is the forty-year period after the end of the American Civil War (1865), named after Mark Twain's book title. The two pictures speak volumes about the thin glittering patina on top of the hoi polloi of New York. In April 1889, **Lafcadio returned to the United States**. He had friends in important places in New York. His closest friend and virtual disciple, was **Elizabeth Bisland**, noted for her charm, beauty and intellect. Several literati were smitten by her, including Rudyard Kipling. Lafcadio kept a picture of her in his study, even after he was married in Japan. Bisland was the literary editor of Cosmopolitan (which was very different from the current fashion magazine).

In the morning of November 14, 1889, Bisland was asked to come to the office of the owner/editor of Cosmopolitan. Without any prior warning she was told to board a train leaving at 6.00 PM for San Francisco and continue her travel around the world "faster than anyone else". At first, she did not like the idea, because she had invited friends for dinner and she did not have proper clothes for a long trip. By 12.00 noon she was convinced, went home, a dressmaker made a suitable outfit and she boarded the train for the scheduled 6.00 PM departure. Of course, such things could only happen in New York and during the Gilded Age.

The editor had read in the morning issue of Pulitzer's New York World newspaper that **Nellie Bly** was leaving that same day, for a trip around the world on a steamship from Hoboken, NJ, towards London. It was really Bly's idea to beat Phileas Fogg record in Jules Verne novel of **"Around the World in Eighty Days"**. Bly was an investigative reporter, she became famous by faking insanity, lived for ten days in an insane asylum and wrote about it. Pulitzer's intervention was required to get her out.

The two women travelled in opposite directions, but the itineraries were almost identical. After San Francisco Bisland sailed to Yokohama/Tokyo, Hong Kong, Singapore, Penang, Ceylon, through the Suez Canal to Brindisi (Italy), by train to Calais (France) and then to New York. Bly had no idea that Bisland was competing against her. When she reached Hong Kong, she visited the steamship company offices and someone told her that another woman was there days earlier travelling west. From Francisco, Bly travelled by a special chartered train and completed the trip in seventy- two days.

Bisland was given misleading information (intentional?) in London and instead of leaving from Southampton on a fast ship she left from Queenstown, Ireland on slow-going Bothnia and completed the journey in seventy-six days. The race was followed closely by millions of Americans, through telegraphic reports in newspapers and magazines.

For my first trip around the world, I flew to Vancouver, then to Tokyo (side trips to Kyoto and Seoul), Hong Kong, Thailand, refueling stop in New Delhi, Rome (side trip to Nice France) and back to Toronto, in May 1983. **It took me a few hours less than eighteen days**.

MONTREAL, CANADA

MONTREAL, Golden Square Mile, late 1880s

First CANADIAN PACIFIC transcontinental train, July 4, 1886

It was a very cold day when Lafcadio arrived in Montreal on March 7, 1890. This is how he described his first impressions in an article published in **Harper's Magazine**

"...[stepped] not upon Canadian soil, but on Canadian ice. Ice many inches thick...lines of sleighs...wait before the station for passengers. No wheeled vehicles...It is quite cold, but beautifully clear...Over the frozen white miles of St. Lawrence [river] sleighs are moving - so far away that it looks like a crawling of beetles". He was on his way to Japan, from New York to Montreal and to Vancouver by train, to board a steamship for Yokohama.

The trip was financed by the legendary Sir William Van Horne, President of **Canadian Pacific (CP) Railway**. Van Horne had managed to complete (1886) the construction of the 3000 km long railway to Vancouver in five years, rather than the ten years planned by the Canadian Government. Van Horne had read at least one of Lafcadio's books and wanted the publishing of good articles about travel experience on CP owned trains and steamships.

Lafcadio left New York and never came back. In Montreal, the 'gilded age' had an ethno-linguistic hue. Anglo-Canadians of Montreal were controlling 75% of the wealth of Canada, with the French-Canadians living mostly in rural Quebec and those in Montreal mostly in lowly positions. The myth was created that all Anglos are rich and the French-speaking folk are all poor. The truth was that the upper crust was only a very small minority. The vast majority had a low standard of living irrespective of their ethno-linguistic origins.

Years later, with the political power firmly in the hands of nationalistic **Quebecois**, strict language laws were passed (from the 1960s on). Among them, the 'sign law' required that all public signage and commercial advertising in Québec must be in French. For example, from a store named YOUNG'S the 's had to be removed. Currently, a relaxed version of the law allows for another language to be used along with French, but "French must be markedly predominant". Two referenda for separation were held and both failed. With globalization, the ultra-nationalistic fervor has subsided.

After the exodus of three hundred thousand Anglos, Montreal has reinvented itself as an even more vibrant city, full of culture and entertainment (city population 1.7 and metro 3.5 million). It is unlike any other in Canada or anywhere else, with 65% Francophones, 15% Anglophones and 20% allophones. Montreal is officially French speaking, but practically bilingual.

Personally, I am used to the Quebecois accent and I enjoy and feel at home speaking French, whenever I visit the city that has so much to offer in education, art, music, festivals and excellent cuisine. Of course, Montreal is best to visit in the summer. However, the Montréalais(e) never shy away from going out in mid winter. There are 32 km of underground Montreal, where salespeople and shoppers do not need to wear much more that a t-shirt or a blouse, even when it is -20 °C above ground.

TORONTO

TORONTO Skyline 2020

Horse-drawn streetcar, downtown Toronto 1890

Lafcadio did not travel through Toronto on his way to Vancouver and Japan, in March 1890. The train route was far to the north, from Montreal towards Lake Superior. If he had come to Toronto, he would have found that his fellow **Irishmen** were the largest ethnic group. Most of them had immigrated to Canada during the Irish Potato Famine (1845-1852). But they were not united, in fact, they were very divided into Protestants and Catholics. Toronto was controlled by the Orange Order, whose members were staunch supporters of Protestantism, of the British Empire and of very conservative values. They hated Catholics and anyone speaking French. All Toronto mayors were protestants and nearly all of them Orangemen till 1954, when Nathan Phillips was elected, who was Jewish. The orange order gradually declined in influence and although there is still an Orange parade on July 12, hardly anyone attends or knows if or where it is being held. However, nearly everybody celebrates Irish heritage and culture on St. Patrick's Day on March 17, irrespective of religious persuasion or ethnic background.

With the influx of immigrants to Toronto (100,000 every year) and English-speaking Canadians from Montreal, Toronto has become both the financial and cultural capital of Canada. In fact, it competes with Chicago for the title of 'Second City' in North America. As former Toronto mayor David Crombie put it "you can get a ticket on the streetcar or the bus and you can go around the world in a day, because in this city we have representation from every language, every racial group, every religious group, every ethnic group that the world has to offer, it's right here in Toronto". I would also add that in Greektown several street names are both in English and Greek (like Danforth Street-ΟΔΟΣ ΝΤΑΝΦΟΡΘ etc.) and in Chinatown Spadina Street etc. are also written in Chinese.

McMaster University, where I have been teaching and doing research since 1968, was named after Senator William McMaster. He was born at Rathnelly, County Tyrone, N. Ireland, immigrated to Canada and acquired his wealth as a merchant and financier, founder of the Canadian Imperial Bank of Commerce. He bequeathed $900,000 (worth about $27 million in todays dollars) for the establishment of 'a school of learning' in Toronto in 1887, which adopted the Greek motto ΤΑ ΠΑΝΤΑ ΕΝ ΧΡΙΣΤΩ ΣΥΝΕΣΤΗΚΕΝ.

McMaster moved to Hamilton (70 km from Toronto) in 1927 and it is now a public research university with about 30,000 undergraduates and 5,000 postgraduate students, ranking among the top 100 universities in the world. Notable faculty and alumni include Bertram Brockhouse (Physics Nobel 1994), Donna Strickland (Physics Nobel 2018, student in my course in Fluid Mechanics in 1979), Myron Scholes (Economics Nobel 1997). Cyrus S. Eaton (graduated in 1905) was a steel and railway capitalist and philanthropist, winner of the Lenin Peace Prize (1960). His Pugwash Conference won the Peace Nobel (1995). Michael Lee-Chin is a billionaire benefactor, student in my course in Fluid Mechanics in 1973.

ALBERTA

The train from Montreal to Vancouver passed by Lake Superior, Winnipeg and the Prairies. Lafcadio in his article published in Harper's Magazine writes "There is not one buffalo now...all have been murdered for their hides......The wanton destruction of the buffalo was the extermination also of a human race. And I have been reading on the train in some Canadian paper, of Indians frenzied by hunger".

Further on he writes "One mountain we pass has **three jagged summits**, with vast clefts between". In fact, Harper's article was accompanied by a black and white picture of the 'Three Sisters', taken almost from the same location as the picture shown. He continues on ".... we reach the loftiest point of the route; we are nearly five thousand three hundred feet above sea [1600 meters].......we descend....the train rocking like a ship as we rush through canyons and gorges and valleys......And it is here, in these canyons and above these chasms, that for the first time one obtains a full sense of the human effort which spanned the northern continent with this wonderful highway of steel, a full comprehension of the enormity of the labour involved". I would add that this 'highway of steel' enabled Canada to become a country spanning from the Atlantic to the Pacific.

The **Canadian Pacific Railway** was built between 1881 and 1886 and Lafcadio travelled in March 1890. The enormous project was accomplished by more than 30,000 labourers and more than 10,000 horses. Many labourers were European immigrants and about 15,000 were Chinese. The Europeans were receiving about double the hourly-pay of the Chinese, who were doing the most dangerous construction jobs. It is estimated that about 1000 Chinese workers died due to accidents or sickness. In 2006 the Canadian government issued a formal apology to the Chinese population in Canada for their treatment both during and following the construction of the Canadian Pacific Railway.

Lafcadio further also wrote about the enormous challenges and dangers of railway construction in the Rockies: "There are certain forms of avalanches against which certain precautions had to be taken, avalanches which rush down one slope with such a fury that the impetus carries them up the opposite slope". It was such a furious avalanche that killed Michel Trudeau (aged 23), youngest son of former Prime Minister Pierre Trudeau and brother of the current Prime Minister Justin Trudeau. Michel was an experienced outdoorsman and he was backcountry skiing when an avalanche swept him into Kokanee Lake, a couple of hundred kilometers southwest of the Three Sisters. Extensive searches by experienced divers were unable to recover his body.

As the train was approaching Vancouver, Lafcadio wrote: "We passed great ranges in the night, and are now steaming through the canyons of the Fraser River. Above us the wooded mountains still lift their snows to the sun. Below us the river runs like a black ribbon edged with white, for it is iced along its edges". I have never travelled by train in that part of Canada, but I have visited the Canadian Rockies. The views are breathtaking.

VANCOUVER

VANCOUVER

SS Abyssinia at
Vancouver harbour

Vancouver was a town of about 15,000 people, when Lafcadio arrived in March 1890. He wrote in his Harper's Magazine article 'A winter Journey to Japan' that Vancouver "is destined to be a mighty city". And he was right: It is now the third largest metropolis in Canada with population of 2.5 million. It is surrounded and fully integrated with nature, due to a superb geographic location and exemplary urban planning. It is perennially listed among the most livable cities in the world, even though it is also one of the most expensive in housing. It is ethnically and linguistically very diverse with about one third of the population Chinese.

The Province of **British Colombia**, was the last to be discovered by the Europeans and was described as 'an immense wilderness at the edge of the world'. The first European to have arrived in this northwest corner of North America was Ioannis Fokas (Ἰωάννης Φωκᾶς) from Kefalonia, Greece, better known by his hispanized name Juan de Fuca. He led a Spanish expedition in 1592 in search of the legendary Northwest Passage, believed to link Atlantic and Pacific. The Juan de Fuca Straight is a 150 km long channel, 20-40 km wide, separating Canada's Vancouver Island, from the USA. The city of Vancouver is not located on the island, but some 50 km across the water.

The fabled **Northwest Passage** remained unnavigable for 400 years and numerous intrepid navigators had tragic end, with Franklin's lost expedition having resulted in 129 deaths. In 1903-1905 Norwegian explorer Roald Amundsen led the first successful expedition, from east to west. It took them over two years to complete the journey as they were learning survival tactics from the local Inuit population.

A large cruise ship, with 1500 passengers, sailed from Vancouver to New York through the Northwest Passage in 28 days, in 2016. Several other cruises were completed ever since and more are planned in 2022 and beyond.

Lafcadio sailed on St. Patrick's Day, March 17, **1890** for Yokohama aboard steamship Abyssinia, which was chartered by Canadian Pacific, the company that had funded his trip. Abyssinia had a speed of 13 knots (24 km/h) and could carry up to 200 first class passengers and 1000 steerage. The picture is from Abyssinia's first trip from Yokohama to Vancouver, in record time of 13 days in June 1887. The steamship caught fire and sank in December of 1891 in the North Atlantic off Nova Scotia, without loss of life.

Vancouver is warmer in the winter and cooler in the summer than other Canadian cities, but it also receives more rain. During a winter visit I was amazed that I could drive to the base of Grouse Mountain in twenty minutes from downtown and then take the gondola to the top for skiing. Once, I also went to Whistler Mountain (about 80 km away), for more challenging ski slopes. Most of the alpine events of the 2010 Winter Olympics were held there.

YOKOHAMA, JAPAN

circa 1890 Grand Hotel, Yokohama

InterContinental
Yokohama Grand
April 2012

The Pacific Ocean voyage to **Yokohama**, lasted 14 days and Lafcadio arrived on April 4, 1890. As the steamship was approaching the port, he saw the magnificent Mount Fuji (aka Fujiyama, Fujisan to Japanese speakers), which stands at 3,776 m (12,389 ft) and it is Japan's highest mountain. Its beautiful symmetrical cone is the symbol of Japan. Japanese are expected to climb Mount Fuji once in their lifetime. It is an active volcano with low eruptive danger (the last eruption occurred in 1707). Mount Fuji is a sacred site for the indigenous **Shinto** religion. Shinto is polytheistic with numerous Kami (deities or spirits). According to Japanese mythology there are 8 million Kami and they inhabit the living, the dead, natural phenomena (like wind, rain, sunshine), volcanoes, trees, rocks, waterfalls and everything else in nature.

In his writings, Lafcadio appears to have been enchanted upon his arrival, even though Japan was in the midst of a disruptive political, economic and social change and not the traditional society of simplicity and charm that he had read about. The island archipelago was completely isolated from the outside world for 250 years, except for Dutch traders who were allowed in the tiny (120mx75m) artificial island of Dejima in the bay of Nagasaki. In was a period of peace but also a period of social stagnation. In the Japanese feudal class system, the merchants were at the bottom of the ladder, artisans above them, then the farmers, with the Samurai at the top ruling by birthright and sword.

However, in July 1853, American Commodore **Matthew C. Perry** arrived in Edo Bay (not far from the Intercontinental Yokohama Grand Hotel) and demanded opening for trade (coal, whale oil and water supply for ships). The presence of the four kurofune (black ships, called so for the billowing black smoke) and the thunder of their guns intimidated the Japanese. The social order was disrupted, rebellions followed, the Shogunate was abolished and the 16-year-old emperor Meiji was brought from Kyoto to Edo (Tokyo). Japan was on high-speed western modernization after the **Meiji Restoration** (revolution) of 1868.

The Grand Hotel was built in 1873. After a devastating earthquake in 1923 it was rebuilt and renamed Hotel New Grand. The principal owner of the Grand was Mitchell MacDonald, a paymaster for the US Navy, Lafcadio's friend who also served as his literary executor after his death. MacDonald perished in the earthquake of 1923. New Grand is where General Douglas MacArthur stayed upon arrival in Japan in 1945, for the first three days. It was commandeered by the Americans 1945-1952 and housed over 100 officers.

The InterContinental Yokohama Grand is about 2 km away also on the waterfront overlooking **Edo (Tokyo) Bay**. I attended a conference at the InterContinental in June 1998 and I remember that its sail-shaped silhouette was easy to spot from far away. On a return visit in 2012 it was dwarfed by higher new buildings nearby.

MATSUE

MATSUE CASTLE, June 2017

Library at Lafcadio Hearn Memorial Museum

Lafcadio Hearn's Old Residence

Matsue, a small coastal city on the Sea of Japan located some 750 km west of Tokyo, was the next stop for Lafcadio. He had obtained a position as a teacher of English with the help of **Basil Hall Chamberlain**, an Englishman and professor of Japanese at Tokyo Imperial University. It was a move away from the nucleus of western modernization to a bucolic part of Japan.

Japan was ruled since the 10th century by the Daimyo, hereditary powerful landholders of vast areas, guarded in their castles by sword-wielding samurai warriors. Tokugawa Ieyasu overpowered all other Daimyo and was formally nominated **Shogun**, by the emperor who had only titular authority. Shoguns were the de facto rulers and in the case of Ieyasu, he became the unifier and absolute ruler of Japan in the early 1600s.

There were 260 Daimyo during the Tokugawa (Edo) period (1603-1868). Each one of them was allowed to have one castle, but no more. Daimyo privileges ended with the Meiji restoration (1868) and the samurais were disbanded. With the loss of privilege many of the castles fell in disrepair. The Matsue Castle is one of the few remaining castles in their original wooden form. It is the second largest in the country and it has been designated with the prestigious title of "National Treasure of Japan".

The arrival (August 1890) of Lafcadio in Matsue was fortuitous destiny. He was destined to become the keeper of Japan's folktales, ghost stories and legends, while the fervent westernizers in Tokyo and Yokohama were too eager to shed Japanese traditions. Lafcadio was very well welcomed in Matsue and he quickly became a local celebrity. Within four months of his arrival 40-year-old Lafcadio got married to **Setsu Koizumi**, 22-year-old daughter of a prominent **samurai family**.

The Koizumis had lost their privileges and fortune with the abolition of the feudal system, after the Meiji restoration. Actually, the samurai fortunes were declining during the 250 years of peace of the Togugawa Shogunate. Warriors were not much needed during the time of peace and the stipends paid to them by the Daimyo were gradually reduced. Lafcadio's salary was good enough for him to move into a nice home in Matsue and live with the entire Koizumi family and their three servants. His residence is a designated historic site open to the public and next to it is the Lafcadio Hearn Memorial Museum.

An exhibition **'The Open Mind of Lafcadio Hearn"** took place at the **Matsue Castle** on October 9-10, 2010, to celebrate 160 years from Lafcadio's birth and 120 years from his arrival in Japan. Among the numerous works of art, a sculpture was unveiled in the presence of the Ambassadors of Greece and Ireland in Japan. The event was coordinated by the spirited team of Takis Efstathiou (fine arts dealer from New York), Bon Koizumi (great-grandson of Lafcadio) and Bon's wife Shoko Koizumi (curator at the Lafcadio Hearn Museum, shown in the picture with me, 2017).

KUMAMOTO

Cherry blossoms at
KUMAMOTO CASTLE

JAPAN

Tokyo

Yokohama

Kobe

Yaizu

Matsue

Lafcadio Hearn's Japan

Kumamoto

Lafcadio wrote "I like everything about Matsue, but I hate the cold weather". The subfreezing winter temperatures at Matsue were hard on his health. He decided to move to a warmer climate. With the help of Professor Basil Hall Chamberlain, he was offered a position to teach English at a school in Kumamoto. The school principal was **Jigoro Kano**, the educator and athlete who founded **Judo**. Lafcadio stayed at Kumamoto for two years. His old residence is now a Museum dedicated to his memory.

Kumamoto is situated in the southwestern island of Kyushu. It is famous in Japan's history for the siege of the castle in 1877. In the years following the Meiji restoration, samurai warriors rebelled against the Meiji government for the loss of privilege. Some 20,000 samurai laid siege at **Kumamoto castle**, which was defended by about 4,000 conscripted soldiers of the Imperial army. The castle withstood the attacks for two months. Eventually large government forces arrived and overwhelmed the samurai attackers.

The leader of the samurai was Saigo Takamori, whose determination and valor inspired the historically inaccurate movie 'The Last Samurai'. Tom Cruise was in the role of an American military officer, while the inspiration came from a Frenchman by the name Jules Brunet. Samurai were fighting with firearms in 1877, while in the Hollywood version of the story they had bows, arrows and body armour belonging to a bygone era.

Kumamoto castle was seriously damaged during the 2016 earthquake (over 200 killed in the surrounding area). Reconstruction is in progress (visitors allowed from 2019). It is expected to be fully restored by 2037. Mount Aso is a large active volcano, near Kumamoto. It erupted in October 2021 (without any injuries or property damage).

Lafcadio was impressed by Jigoro Kano's personality and knowledge of Japanese martial arts. He wrote an essay on **judo** referring to it as jiujutsu, apparently because the word judo was not known outside a small circle of practitioners. Lafcadio's article helped popularize the sport in Europe and the Americas. An incident was widely caricatured, about a suffragette of small stature throwing a beefy policeman to the ground, during a demonstration for the right of women to vote.

As explained in a judo manual "resisting a more powerful opponent will result in your defeat, whilst adjusting to and evading your opponent's attack will cause him to lose his balance, his power will be reduced, and you will defeat him". In fact, judo is more than just a sport, it is also a philosophy of life and work. Apparently, some enthusiasts use Judo techniques in their professional activities.

I was supposed to visit Kumamoto in April 2021, postponed for April 2022, in connection with a Polymer Processing Society conference in nearby Fukuoka. Unfortunately, my plans were thwarted by the recent upsurge of the pandemic and I gave my talk online, from my home.

KOBE

KOBE Waterfront

PPS-5 April 1989
Banquet
KYOTO

Lafcadio had published two books, 'Glimpses of Unfamiliar Japan' and 'Out of the East', before moving to Kobe in 1894 to work for Kobe Chronicle, an English-language newspaper. Kobe is located on the north shore of Osaka Bay. Nowadays **Osaka, Kobe** and **Kyoto** form a metropolitan area of about 23 million people, in the centrally located **Kansai region**. Kyoto was the imperial capital till the Meiji restoration (1868), when Edo was renamed Tokyo (which means east(ern)-capital).

Lafcadio became a Japanese citizen while he was in Kobe. In fact, he is the first foreigner ever to become naturalized citizen of Japan. Other foreigners had lived and died in Japan in the past. However, the first (Meiji) Constitution of unified Japan was signed just prior to Lafcadio's arrival. He took the family name of his samurai wife, **KOIZUMI (小泉),** and for his first name he chose **YAKUMO (八雲).** Yakumo means 'eight clouds'. Why eight? Probably because eight is the luckiest number in Japan (and in China). The unluckiest number is four (pronounced shi), which sounds like the word for death, in both Japanese and Chinese.

Kyoto is also the capital of Japanese traditions. Here is how Lafcadio describes a Geisha in his first book on Japan: "She is taught etiquette, grace, polite speech, she has daily lessons in dancing, and she is obliged to learn by heart a multitude of songs............ she is taught to handle musical instruments.........knows how to fill your wine-cup exactly full, with a single toss of the bottle and without spilling a drop, between two taps of her drum". In just about every conference banquet that I have attended in Japan, there was a Geisha dancing, as part of the entertainment program. Young Japanese colleagues were rather unhappy with the presence of a Geisha.

My first visit to Kobe was in November 1992 for a presentation at a conference of the Society of Rheology, Japan. My hotel was conveniently located at the central (Sannomiya) railway station and the conference was held at the convention center on an artificial island. Every day I would take a driverless train over the harbor waters to reach it. I must say that I had an uneasy feeling during the 6 km trip, knowing of the frequent earthquakes in Japan.

Kobe was devastated by a **strong earthquake** on January 17, 1995, early in the morning. Over 6,000 people perished. On a return visit in June 2006, I was unable to locate the building of my hotel or recognize any of the surroundings, even though I had stayed for ten days and I used to jog daily at a nearby park in 1992. According to a report regarding the rail line to the convention center "Five of the nine stations along the line suffered various degrees of damage. One concrete column near the Sannomiya station was seriously sheared and dropped"

KYOTO

KYOTO

ある英語教師の思い出
小泉八雲の次男・稲垣巌の生涯

小野木重治 編著

Lafcadio's son
Iwao Inagaki
by S. Onogi

小泉八雲研究の空白を埋める──！

小泉八雲の次男・巌（いわお）は、幼時より母セツの生家の継嗣となって姓が変わり、四十歳の若さで夭逝した。本書は、その知られざる生涯を、かつて教鞭をとった京都府立桃山中学時代の同僚や教え子たちの回想によって浮き彫りにする。

恒文社刊・定価2,500円（本体2,427円）

Japan, May 1983

I took the **Shinkansen "bullet train"** on May 6, 1983 from Tokyo to Kyoto and the duration of the trip was a bit over two hours for the 450 km distance. The names of the Sinkansen trains are interesting: Kodama (echo) stops at every station. Hikari (light) is a semi fast train and the fastest Nozomi (hope) stops at main stations only. Current maximum operating speed is 320 km/h.

I presented a seminar at Kyoto University. My host was **professor Shigeharu Onogi** (1920-2015), the 'father' of rheology in Japan. He took me to see Sanjunsangendo Temple (means "33 intervals" that is 34 columns), which features 1001 statues of Kannon, the goddess of mercy. What I did not know, at the time, was that Professor Onogi had as a teacher of English the second son of Lafcadio and wrote a 237-page book about him. What a coincidence! During my first trip to Japan, I was just two 'degrees of separation' from Lafcadio. The book cover reads: Memory of an English teacher. The second son of Koizumi Yakumo. Life of Inagaki Iwao.

Kyoto was the imperial capital of Japan from 794 to 1868 (Meiji restoration). It is still considered the capital of Japanese culture and tradition. The Emperor of Japan had only nominal power, with de facto ruler being the Shogun. According to Japanese mythology the first imperial court was established in 660 BC. Documented historical references exist from some thousand years later. The emperor is the head of the pantheistic Shinto religion. He is considered to be a direct descendant of Amaterasu, the goddess of the sun. Hirohito was the **Emperor of Japan** (grandson of Meiji) before, during and after World War II.

General Douglas MacArthur was the de facto absolute monarch for six years (1945-1951) and was nicknamed Gaijin Shōgun (foreign Shogun). He stage-managed the end of the war, occupation and re-inventing of Japan in a very skilful way. He was aware that politeness, generosity, saving face and traditions were very important in Japanese society. He took no actions against the emperor, even though some Washington politicians were urging him to "hang Hirohito" as a war criminal. He did not debase him in any shape or form. The re-making of Japan was a roaring success.

Seven books of Lafcadio were found in MacArthur's personal library after his death. It is not known whether he had the time to do much reading before or during the occupation of Japan. However, behind the great general was a smart intelligence officer. He was **Brigadier General Bonner Fellers**, chief of psychological warfare in the staff of the Supreme Commander of the Allied Powers (MacArthur). Fellers was an admirer of Hearn and had visited Japan on several occasions to write his graduate thesis on "Psychology of the Japanese soldier" (1934). He had befriended members of the Koizumi family. In fact, Lafcadio's great-grandson Bon Koizumi was named after him.

HIMEJI and OSAKA

Himeji Castle
September 1986

OSAKA

Himeji is located at the western end of the Kansai region (about 550 km from Tokyo). It was my second trip to Japan, when I visited Himeji for lecturing at a large chemical corporation. After the lectures, my hosts took me to see the beautiful castle. From about 100 castles in Japan, **Himeji Castle** is the largest and most visited of them all.

Lafcadio retold a Japanese legend about Himeji, in his inimitable writing style. It was about a young girl serving as a maid in a castle. However, when one of ten golden dishes disappeared from the household, the girl committed suicide to prove her innocence. Her name was Kiku, which is the word for **chrysanthemum**. The flower represents Japan's imperial throne and the nation. However, it is considered bad luck to grow chrysanthemums in Himeji, due to the tragic ending of the girl. According to the legend her ghost returns every night and counts the golden dishes.

Pre-modern history of Japan starts in **1543**, when three Portuguese navigators arrived at the island of Tanegashima. The local warlord was very impressed by their firearms. He purchased one and gave it to a craftsman to reproduce it. The initial reproduction efforts were not very successful. A year later the Portuguese came back accompanied by a gun maker and quickly firearms were produced in Japan in large quantities. The Kansai region and the surrounding area was the scene of several battles during the turbulent civil war years of the late 1500s.

Three leaders emerged, known as the unifiers: Oda Nobunaga, Toyotomi Hideyoshi (owned Himeji Castle) and **Tokugawa Ieyasu**. They were radically different in character, as illustrated in a story known by all Japanese schoolchildren: The three unifiers were watching a cuckoo bird and waiting for it to sing, but the bird wouldn't sing. Nobunaga says "Little bird, if you don't sing, I will kill you". Hideyoshi says "Little bird, if you don't sing, I'll make you sing". Then Ieyasu says "Little bird, if you don't sing, I will wait for you to sing". Tokugawa Ieyasu, with his patience, shrewdness and loyal samurai warriors, defeated and outlasted all his rivals. He gave Himeji castle to his son-in-law as a reward for his loyalty.

While Himeji and Kyoto are steeped in history and tradition, **Osaka** is famous for modernity, shopping and dining. I have heard that when people in Osaka meet, the standard greeting is "mokarimakka", which literally means "are you making good money?" Heaven forbid uttering that in Tokyo. Another expression related to Osaka is "kui-daore" which means "eat till you go bankrupt". Lafcadio, back in 1895, when he visited Osaka, he discovered a comfortable cohabitation of tradition and modernity. Perhaps the same can be said for today. In a city dominated by neon lights, designer brands and fine restaurants, there is also a beautiful castle and several temples worth visiting.

MOUNT FUJI

Lafcadio climbed **Mount Fuli** (aka Fujiyama, **Fujisan** to Japanese speakers) together with a former student from Matsue, in August 1897. I visited Mount Fuji in December 1999. With high school friend Spyros Aliagas, who was serving as the First Secretary of the Greek Embassy in Tokyo, we drove to the Fuji Subaru Line 5th station (2305 meters altitude). We did not attempt to go any higher. Ascent to the top (3776 m, 12,389 ft) would require at least 6 hours of walking uphill along a volcanic rock trail. In the summer months, around 10,000 people ascend to the top every day.

Fujisan is a sacred mountain for the indigenous **Shinto** religion. Shinto is polytheistic (or pantheistic) with numerous deities called Kami. The Kami (goddess) of Mount Fuji is a mythological princess, whose symbol is cherry blossom (sakura). **Buddhism** also is practiced and although most Japanese do not identify as religious, they take part in Shinto (69%) and Buddhist (67%) activities and festivities. The sum is more than 100%, because many Japanese practice both faiths. Believers pray at separate holy sites: Shrines (jinja) are Shinto sites of worship and temples (tera) are Buddhist.

Shinto originated in Japan. Buddhism has its origins in India and came to Japan from China. Shinto is really worship of nature. Buddhism does not include belief in a creator and almighty god. The teachings are ideas and training of humans to achieve enlightenment. Lafcadio in his book *'Japan's Religions: Shinto and Buddhism'* explains the philosophical foundations and how the two faiths influenced each other.

Jesuit and other Catholic missionaries arrived in Japan soon after the Portuguese landed in the southwestern island of Tanegashima, in 1543. Numerous Japanese were converted to **Christianity**. However, most Daimyo warlords thought that Christianity was destabilizing the social order in the country.

In 1600 Englishman William Adams and his Dutch shipmate Jan Joosten were two survivors (both Protestants), of a Dutch trading expedition, who landed in Kyusu. They were quickly arrested and imprisoned. Portuguese Jesuits suggested that they were pirates and ought to be executed. Shogun Tokugawa Ieyasu questioned them and realized that there is a lot to learn about the West from them. They were not permitted to leave and they settled in Japan.

From William Adams, Ieyasu heard that Catholicism is not the only religion in Europe, as the Jesuit missionaries claimed. After 1614 the practice of Christianity was banned, missionaries were expelled and numerous Christians were executed. An **isolationist policy**, called **Sakoku** (locked country), was implemented from 1603 to 1854. The popular TV miniseries Shogun (1980), with Richard Chamberlain in the lead role, is a fictionalized version of William Adams adventures

TOKYO I

Lafcadio obtained a position as professor of English literature at Tokyo Imperial University, with the help of Basil Chamberlain, in 1896 and remained there till 1903. Tokyo's population was more than 1 million, too large for Lafcadio's taste. At present, the greater Tokyo area has a population of 38 million and it is the world's largest metropolis. Lafcadio Hearn Park is located in Nishi-Shinjuku. Note the symbolism of the flowers and the sign in Japanese and Greek: Red and white are the colours of the Japanese flag.

It was during my third (of 15 trips) to Japan when I fully realized how important Lafcadio was for Japanese folklore and culture. In April of 1989, after a flight from Athens to Frankfurt and then a 13-hour flight to Narita airport, I arrived in Tokyo. I was very tired when I reached Sinjuku Prince Hotel and I fell quickly asleep. A couple of hours later, I was awakened due to loud Greek spoken on a Japanese TV station that I had accidentally left on. Next morning, I read in Japan Times, Tokyo's English language newspaper, that a delegation from Lefcada had arrived for signing a "sister city" agreement with Shinjuku. A day later I lectured at a Mitsubishi research center. At dinner time I asked my hosts if they knew about Lafcadio's writings. They told me that Japanese folktales, written in English by Lafcadio, were translated and taught in all schools in Japan. Everyone knew a lot about Lafcadio and his writings!

I left Tokyo to give another lecture at another Mitsubishi company near Osaka. When I returned, I stayed at a hotel near the famous **Tokyo Eki** (railway station). It was Saturday evening and I went out for a late-night dinner at the tree-lined Omotesando Dori (avenue), which is the most westernized part of Tokyo. When I decided to return to my hotel, it was about 1.00 AM after the subway trains had stopped. In vain, I waited for half an hour to catch a taxi. All taxis were occupied and driving away. With a few Japanese words I could master, I managed to ask a policeman. He told me that I should not expect to catch a taxi before 4.00 AM. Tokyo is the safest large city in the world and I decided to walk back to my hotel, knowing that I needed at least hour-and-an-half. Luckily, I caught a taxi half way.

In 1989 the Japanese economy was at the peak of its boom. April is **sakura** (cherry blossoms) time in Japan and millions of people were going out to restaurants, bars, theaters and other entertainment venues. When I went back to Tokyo, in November of 1992, things were different. It was a year after the economic bubble had burst. No problem catching a taxi from Omotesando avenue at any time of day or night. By the way, an annual Saint Patrick's day parade takes place along Omodesando, with at least 15,000 participants and 50,000 spectators. The distance from Ireland gives a new meaning to the Irish song "it's a long way from Tipperary"

TOKYO II

Japan's modern history started in **1868** when 16-year-old **emperor Meiji** was brought from Kyoto to Edo (Tokyo). Lafcadio remained in Japan from his arrival in 1890 till his death in 1904. It was during the Meiji period (1868-1912) when Japan experienced a tsunami of modernization or, better said, westernization. Lafcadio, through his writings, became the keeper of Japan's folktales and traditions and interpreter of Japanese spirit. That is why he is honored with several memorials throughout Japan, including his bust at Nishi-Shinjuku.

By the 1890s, Japan was technologically advanced, militarily very strong and was victorious during the First Sino-Japanese War (1894-1895). This victory established Japan as the predominant power in the Far East. The Russo-Japanese War (1904-1905) started with the naval battle of Port Arthur and ended after the Russians suffered a humiliating defeat.

In 1931 Japan invaded Manchuria and during the Second Sino-Japanese War (1937-1945) other parts of China. From 1940 Japan was, one of the Axis powers, with Germany and Italy. On December 7, 1941, Japan carried out a surprise attack against the US naval base at **Pearl Harbor**, in Honolulu, Hawaii. Several US ships were badly damaged, 188 aircraft were destroyed and 2403 Americans were killed. The US retaliated with the "Doolittle raid" of 16 planes that bombed Yokohama and Tokyo on April 18, 1942. It was planned and led by Colonel (later General) James Doolittle, whom I happened to meet in person, when he delivered a seminar, at Washington University in St. Louis in 1966.

During the Pacific War, fierce battles took place in several parts of Asia and the islands of the Pacific Ocean, with enormous losses in human lives. In the night of March 9-10,1945, the US Air Force carried out several firebombing raids on Tokyo with three hundred B-29s, which left about 100,000 dead and over 1 million homeless. But there were no signs that Japan would surrender. Invasion plans were underway. President Truman after hearing from General Douglas MacArthur, that American casualties could exceed 1 million, he decided to order nuclear bombing on Hiroshima (August 6) and Nagasaki (August 9). The unconditional surrender of Japan was announced by Emperor Hirohito, on August 15, 1945.

General Douglas MacArthur became the absolute ruler of Japan (1945-1951). He had set up his headquarters in the Dai-Ichi Building across from the Imperial Palace. Japan experienced an unprecedented economic growth from the end of World War II to 1991. Japanese management practices were extolled in numerous books, which are no longer popular. It was not the management style, but the capacity of Japanese people to work diligently for long hours that led to prosperity.

TOKYO III

Japanese tea ceremony at Happo-en Garden
September 1986

HAPPO-EN, Shirokanedai, TOKYO

This is what Lafcadio wrote in one of his books: "The **tea ceremony** requires years of training and practice ... yet the whole of this art, as to its detail, signifies no more than the making and serving of a cup of tea. The supremely important matter is that the act be performed in the most perfect, most polite, most graceful, most charming manner possible". It was in September of 1986, in connection with two conferences in Tokyo, that I was invited to take part in a tea ceremony.

Another expression of politeness, manner and etiquette is **bowing**. A few days before the tea ceremony, I was at Keio Plaza Hotel, located in the heart of Tokyo, for the World Congress III of Chemical Engineering. During the opening reception I met a Japanese colleague, who was the director of an industrial research laboratory. We were joined by a third person whom I did not know and we were talking about the congress. At some point, I noticed that the three of us were left alone at the center of the large ballroom and the other congress delegates were outside of a circle of at least 20 feet (6 meters) in radius. Japanese persons crossing the circle were bowing deeply in a very ceremonial manner.

Bowing is a fundamental part of Japanese culture. It is a salutation and expression of respect and social rank. The body must be bent at the waist keeping the back completely straight. Many corporations in Japan train their employees on proper bowing etiquette in business meetings. The bowing that was obviously directed to one of the three of us, appeared to be deeper than I had ever witnessed. The "third" person ought to be of very high professional rank, I thought. I asked and was told that he was Mr. Yasuoki Takeuchi, President of Nippon Oil, a huge petroleum conglomerate with dozens of fully or partly owned subsidiaries and with tens of thousands of employees.

Bowing is a widespread Japanese tradition which has originated from the samurai. It is part of their Bushido (code of honor, moral behavior and lifestyle). Over the years it has trickled down to the three lower social classes: farmers, artisans and merchants. The Japanese tea ceremony is closely affiliated with Zen Buddhism. Like flower arrangement and ceremonial incense appreciation, it is considered as an art of refinement.

Perhaps it is difficult for westerners to fully comprehend why such practices are part of Japanese identity and spirit. To understand more, I would recommend Lafcadio Hearn's book '*Japan: An Attempt at Interpretation*'. It is downloadable for free in various formats, from Gutenberg.org. This book includes chapters on strangeness and charm, Shinto, Buddhism, rise of the military power, family, social organization and more. By the way, the Gutenberg.org website includes 35 other open access books written by or about Lafcadio.

TSUNAMI

Lafcadio in his book *'Gleanings in Buddha-Fields'* (published in 1897) wrote "From immemorial time the shores of Japan have been swept, at irregular intervals of centuries, by enormous tidal waves, tidal waves caused by earthquakes or by submarine volcanic action. These awful sudden risings of the sea are called by the Japanese **tsunami**. The last one occurred on the evening of **June 17, 1896**, when a wave nearly two hundred miles long struck the northeastern provinces of Miyagi, Iwaté, and Aomori, wrecking scores of towns and villages, ruining whole districts, and destroying nearly thirty thousand human lives".

It was the first time that the word **tsunami** was introduced in the English language. He went on to write about Hamaguchi Goryo (Gohei, in Lafcadio's book) a village headman in Hirogawa, south of Osaka. In **1854** after an earthquake, which did not appear to be terribly strong, Hamaguchi noticed that the sea "was running away from land". Many villagers ran to the beach to watch the strange phenomenon.

Hamaguchi realized that a tsunami wave would follow and asked his grandson to light quickly a pine-torch for him. He then started torching his entire rice harvest, which was in sun-dried sheaves ready for transportation to market. His grandson and the villagers thought that Hamaguchi had gone mad. They ran to the hilltop to extinguish the huge fire. The tsunami waves struck with devastating force, but nearly all of the 400 villagers were saved. This was the world's first early warning 'system' for a tsunami. The illustration is from a Government of Japan book for tsunami awareness among children.

In early afternoon, on **March 11, 2011**, a mega-earthquake of magnitude 9.1 shook Japan for 6 minutes. The epicenter was in the Pacific Ocean north east of Tokyo. The resulting tsunami waves, travelling at 700 km/h and up to 40 meters high, smashed on the coast near Sendai. More than 20,000 people were killed and about 2500 went missing. The Fukushima Daiichi Nuclear Power Plant suffered meltdown in three nuclear reactors. It was due to failure of emergency generators, which were powering pumps for cooling water. Radioactivity was released in the surrounding area.

I was supposed to be in Tokyo during the tsunami of March 11, 2011. However, due to another professional commitment in Canada, I changed my original travel plans and visited Japan two weeks earlier. My return flight from Tokyo to Toronto was in early afternoon on February 27.

A business associate of mine told me that travelling by public or private transportation in the Tokyo/ Yokohama area (38 million people), was extremely difficult after the tsunami. It took him three days to reach his home (by walking, taxi, bus and train), for a trip that otherwise would be no more than two-three hours.

YAMAGATA AND KANAZAWA

PPS-22, Yamagata, July 2006

Kanazawa University, February 2011

Lafcadio in his 'Japan: An attempt at interpretation' writes "Nothing is more silent than the beginning of a **Japanese banquet**, and no one, except a native, who observes the opening scene could possibly imagine the tumultuous ending...Then, all at once , with a little burst of laughter, a number of young girls enter, make the customary prostration greeting...They are pretty, they are clad in very costly robes of silk. These are the geisha or dancing girls hired for the banquet......two girls dancing together with such coincidence of step and gesture as only years of training could render possible....dancing-acting accompanied with extraordinary waving of sleeves and fans".

Lafcadio's description could also be for the banquet of the Polymer Processing Society 22nd annual conference (PPS-22). But the beginning was not silent as more than half of several hundred guests were not Japanese. The foldable hand fans are part of geisha attire, especially for dancing performances. Hand fans have been around in Japan for thousand years. Originally, they were used by the samurai as a material to write on.

Yamagata is located north east of Tokyo, some 50 kilometers west from Sendai. It is inland and it was not affected by the March 11, 2011, devastating tsunami. During the conference, in addition to the scientific presentations, we had a very nice talk about Ryokan (Japanese traditional inns). They usually feature tatami mats, futon beds and Japanese-style baths. I have stayed once at a Ryokan and enjoyed it very much.

I travelled to **Kanazawa** to present a seminar at the Polymer Physics laboratory, in February 2011. The weather was rather mild in Tokyo. I took the shinkansen train and an hour or so later, after a long tunnel, I saw incredible amounts of snow. The landscape looked more like Canada than Japan. We were passing near Nagano, where the 1998 winter Olympics were held. Kanazawa (population about 500,000) is a city which features prominently in Japanese history. I saw a lot of expertly crafted samurai body armour and helmets at the local museum.

Lafcadio gives an excellent interpretation of samurai personality and character by describing one of his students "Ishihara is a samurai a very influential lad in his class because of his uncommon force of character. Compared with others, he has a somewhat brusque, independent manner, pleasing, however, by its honest manliness. He says everything he thinks, and precisely in the tone that he thinks it, even to the degree of being a little embarrassing sometimes. He does not hesitate, for example, to find fault with a teacher's method of explanation, and to insist upon a more lucid one. He has criticized me more than once; but I never found that he was wrong". Lafcadio's wife was from a samurai family and he took their name: Koizumi

YAIZU

Mount Fuji view from Yaizu

Shinto Shrine in Yaizu

Lafcadio was not happy with the hassle and bustle of Tokyo which in the late 1890s had a population of over a million people. In the summer of 1897, he visited **Yaizu**, a small fishing village, and immediately he fell in love with it.

Lafcadio was fond of swimming. He was too young, when he left **Lefcada**, to remember the Ionian Sea waterfront, unless it was some kind of subconscious connection. Perhaps Yaizu reminded him of his summer vacations at **Tramore** in Ireland, when he was growing up. It could also be the memories from New Orleans and Martinique that made him love the sound of waves crashing on a beach. However, his wife, Setsu, was not fond of the living accommodations for her, Lafcadio and their four children.

Undoubtedly, the spectacular view of Mount Fuji and importance of the volcano in the Shinto religion was also exercising a magnetic attraction. He kept coming to Yaizu for his summer vacations till his death in the Fall of **1904**.

Here is what Lafcadio wrote in his book ***Japan, An Attempt at Interpretation***', probably while he was in Yaizu.

"The majority of the first impressions of Japan recorded by travellers are pleasurable impressions. Indeed, there must be something lacking, or something very harsh, in the nature to which Japan can make no emotional appeal. The appeal itself is the clue to a problem; and that problem is the character of a race and of its civilization.

My own first impressions of Japan, Japan as seen in the white sunshine of a perfect spring day,-had doubtless much in common with the average of such experiences. I remember especially the wonder and the delight of the vision. The wonder and the delight have never passed away: they are often revived for me even now, by some chance happening, after fourteen years of sojourn. But the reason of these feelings was difficult to learn, or at least to guess; for I cannot yet claim to know much about Japan. . . . Long ago the best and dearest Japanese friend I ever had said to me, a little before his death: "When you find, in four or five years more, that you cannot understand the Japanese at all, then you will begin to know something about them." After having realized the truth of my friend's prediction, after having discovered that I cannot understand the Japanese at all, I feel better qualified to attempt this essay."

VOLOS, GREECE

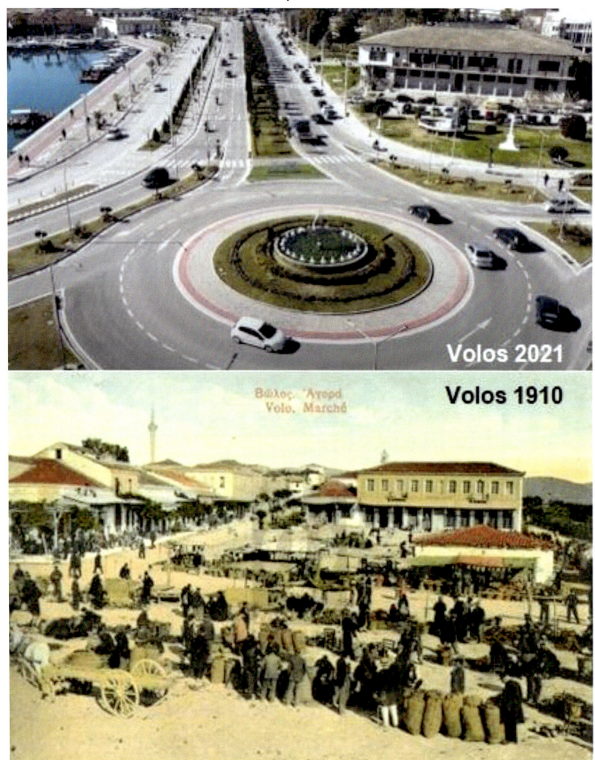

Volos 2021

Volos 1910

Volos is situated some 300 kilometers North of Athens and 200 kilometers south of Thessaloniki, at the foot of Mount Pelion on the coast of Pagasitic Gulf of the Aegean Sea. The municipality had a population of about 5,000 when it was first incorporated into the independent Kingdom of Greece in 1881, after nearly 500 years of Ottoman rule. Currently it has a population of about 150,000.

Modern Volos occupies the areas of ancient Iolkos, Pagasae and Demetrias. Iolkos is the homeland of mythological hero **Jason** and the **Argonauts**. They sailed to Colchis, located in the east coast of the Black Sea, in modern Georgia. Their mission was to get possession of the golden fleece and bring it back to Greece. In his quest for the Golden Fleece, Jason was aided by princess Medea. She fled with Jason and they settled in Corinth. Jason did not keep his vows of eternal love to Medea and abandoned her for the daughter of the king of Corinth, Creusa. Medea, though sorcery, killed Creusa and fearing that her children will be enslaved she killed them too.

Mount Pelion is the land Centaurs, the mythological creatures having the upper body of a man and lower body and legs of horse. Mount Pelion took its name from Peleus the father of **Achilles**. It is on mount Pelion that an uninvited goddess tossed a golden apple (μῆλον τῆς Ἔριδος, apple of discord) with the inscription "τῇ καλλίστῃ" (to the most beautiful) in the wedding feast of Peleus to Thetis. Paris the son of the king of Troy acted as a judge in the vanity-fueled dispute between the goddesses Hera (Juno), Athena (Minerva) and Aphrodite (Venus). His judgement in favor of goddess Aphrodite led to the Trojan war.

I was born and finished high school in Volos. I studied Chemical Engineering at NTUA (Εθνικό Μετσόβιο Πολυτεχνείο, ΕΜΠ) in Athens and subsequently I received a Master's and a Doctorate from Washington University, St. Louis, Mo (USA). I joined the Department of Chemical Engineering at McMaster University, in Hamilton, Ontario, Canada, as an assistant professor a month before my twenty sixth birthday. I was promoted through the ranks, served as Department Chair for three years and now I am professor emeritus (retired from teaching, but active in research and professional services).

To present the results of my research, I took part in numerous scientific conferences and lectured around the world in seven languages (mostly in English, several times in Greek, German, French and Spanish, twelve hours in Italian and three hours in Portuguese. In parallel with my university teaching and research I have been providing consulting services, supplying computer software packages to polymer processing corporations and teaching courses to their engineers.

Niagara Falls is located 70 km away from my home in Burlington (population 200,000). The Lake Ontario waterfront is less than 250 meters, diagonally and across North Shore Boulevard East. McMaster University is located in Hamilton (population 500,000) 15 kilometers away. Toronto (metro population 6.2 million) is about 60 kilometers from Burlington.

Winters are cold (but rarely below -20 °C) and dry, summers can be hot (up to 38 °C) and humid. The Burlington waterfront is where I do my daily hour-long walk.